DIARY 2024

2024 YEAR PLANNER

The year 2024 (MMXXIV) will be a leap year starting on Monday of the Gregorian calendar.

JANUARY

M	T	W	T	F	S	S
1	2	3	4	5	6	7
8	9	10	11	12	13	14
15	16	17	18	19	20	21
22	23	24	25	26	27	28
29	30	31				

FEBRUARY

M	T	W	T	F	S	S
			1	2	3	4
5	6	7	8	9	10	11
12	13	14	15	16	17	18
19	20	21	22	23	24	25
26	27	28	29			

MARCH

M	T	W	T	F	S	S
				1	2	3
4	5	6	7	8	9	10
11	12	13	14	15	16	17
18	19	20	21	22	23	24
25	26	27	28	29	30	31

APRIL

M	T	W	T	F	S	S
1	2	3	4	5	6	7
8	9	10	11	12	13	14
15	16	17	18	19	20	21
22	23	24	25	26	27	28
29	30					

MAY

M	T	W	T	F	S	S
		1	2	3	4	5
6	7	8	9	10	11	12
13	14	15	16	17	18	19
20	21	22	23	24	25	26
27	28	29	30	31		

JUNE

M	T	W	T	F	S	S
					1	2
3	4	5	6	7	8	9
10	11	12	13	14	15	16
17	18	19	20	21	22	23
24	25	26	27	28	29	30

JULY

M	T	W	T	F	S	S
1	2	3	4	5	6	7
8	9	10	11	12	13	14
15	16	17	18	19	20	21
22	23	24	25	26	27	28
29	30	31				

AUGUST

M	T	W	T	F	S	S
			1	2	3	4
5	6	7	8	9	10	11
12	13	14	15	16	17	18
19	20	21	22	23	24	25
26	27	28	29	30	31	

SEPTEMBER

M	T	W	T	F	S	S
						1
2	3	4	5	6	7	8
9	10	11	12	13	14	15
16	17	18	19	20	21	22
23	24	25	26	27	28	29
30						

OCTOBER

M	T	W	T	F	S	S
	1	2	3	4	5	6
7	8	9	10	11	12	13
14	15	16	17	18	19	20
21	22	23	24	25	26	27
28	29	30	31			

NOVEMBER

M	T	W	T	F	S	S
				1	2	3
4	5	6	7	8	9	10
11	12	13	14	15	16	17
18	19	20	21	22	23	24
25	26	27	28	29	30	

DECEMBER

M	T	W	T	F	S	S
						1
2	3	4	5	6	7	8
9	10	11	12	13	14	15
16	17	18	19	20	21	22
23	24	25	26	27	28	29
30	31					

Did you know?

Between July 26th and August 11th, the 2024 Summer Olympics will taken place in Paris, France

NAMES AND ADDRESSES

INTERNATIONAL DIALING CODES

Afghanistan	+93	Chad	+235
Albania	+355	Chile	+56
Algeria	+213	China	+86
Andorra	+376	Colombia	+57
Angola	+244	Comoros	+269
Argentina	+54	Cook Islands	+682
Armenia	+374	Costa Rica	+506
Aruba	+297	Côte D'Ivoire	+225
Australia	+61	Croatia	+385
Austria	+43	Cuba	+53
Azerbaijan	+994	Cyprus	+357
Bahamas	+1	Czech Rep	+420
Bahrain	+973	Denmark	+45
Bangladesh	+880	Djibouti	+253
Belarus	+375	Ecuador	+593
Belgium	+32	Egypt	+20
Belize	+501	Eritrea	+291
Benin	+229	Estonia	+372
Bhutan	+975	Ethiopia	+251
Bolivia	+591	Falklands	+500
Botswana	+267	Faroe Islands	+298
Brazil	+55	Fiji	+679
Bulgaria	+359	Finland	+358
Burundi	+257	France	+33
Cambodia	+855	Georgia	+995
Cameroon	+237	Germany	+49
Canada	+1	Ghana	+233
Cape Verde	+238	Gibraltar	+350

Greece	+30	Malaysia	+60
Greenland	+299	Malta	+356
Guatemala	+502	Mexico	+52
Guinea	+224	Monaco	+377
Guyana	+592	Nepal	+977
Haiti	+509	Netherlands	+31
Honduras	+504	New Zealand	+64
Hong Kong	+852	Nigeria	+234
Hungary	+36	Norway	+47
Iceland	+354	Pakistan	+92
India	+91	Panama	+507
Indonesia	+62	Paraguay	+595
Iran	+98	Peru	+51
Iraq	+964	Philippines	+63
Ireland	+353	Poland	+48
Israel	+972	Portugal	+351
Italy	+39	Qatar	+974
Japan	+81	Russia	+7
Kazakhstan	+7	Singapore	+65
Kenya	+254	South Africa	+27
Korea (N)	+850	Spain	+34
Korea (S)	+82	Sweden	+46
Kuwait	+965	Switzerland	+41
Kyrgyzstan	+996	Thailand	+66
Latvia	+371	Ukraine	+380
Lebanon	+961	UAE	+971
Libya	+218	UK	+44
Lithuania	+370	USA	+1
Luxembourg	+352	Uruguay	+598
Madagascar	+261	Zambia	+260

JANUARY 2024

Week 1

Did you know?
Euro 2024 will take place from 14th June to 14th July in Germany.

Monday   1

Tuesday   2

Wednesday   3

Thursday 4

Friday 5

Saturday 6

Sunday 7

JANUARY 2024

Week 2

Monday   8

Tuesday   9

Wednesday 10

Thursday   11

Friday 12

Saturday 13

Sunday 14

JANUARY 2024

Week 3

Monday   15

Tuesday   16

Wednesday 17

Thursday   18

Friday   19

Saturday   20

Sunday   21

JANUARY 2024

Week 4

Monday   22

Tuesday   23

Wednesday 24

Thursday   25

Friday   26

Saturday   27

Sunday   28

JANUARY 2024

Week 5

Monday   29

Tuesday   30

Wednesday 31

FEBRUARY 2024

Thursday   1

Friday   2

Saturday   3

Sunday   4

FEBRUARY 2024
Week 6

Monday   5

Tuesday   6

Wednesday   7

Thursday   8

Friday   **9**

Saturday   **10**

Sunday   **11**

FEBRUARY 2024

Week 7

Monday   12

Tuesday   13

Wednesday 14

Thursday   15

Friday   16

Saturday   17

Sunday   18

FEBRUARY 2024
Week 8

Monday   19

Tuesday   20

Wednesday 21

Thursday   22

Friday   **23**

Saturday   **24**

Sunday   **25**

FEBRUARY 2024

Week 9

Monday   26

Tuesday   27

Wednesday 28

Thursday   29

MARCH 2024

Friday 1

Saturday 2

Sunday 3

MARCH 2024

Week 10

Monday   4

Tuesday   5

Wednesday   6

Thursday   7

Friday 8

Saturday 9

Sunday 10

MARCH 2024

Week 11

Monday   11

Tuesday   12

Wednesday 13

Thursday   14

Friday   15

Saturday   16

Sunday   17

MARCH 2024

Week 12

Monday   18

Tuesday   19

Wednesday 20

Thursday   21

Friday 22

Saturday 23

Sunday 24

MARCH 2024

Week 13

Monday   25

Tuesday   26

Wednesday 27

Thursday   28

Friday   **29**

Saturday   **30**

Sunday   **31**

APRIL 2024

Week 14

Monday 1

Tuesday 2

Wednesday 3

Thursday 4

Friday   5

Saturday   6

Sunday   7

APRIL 2024

Week 15

Monday   8

Tuesday   9

Wednesday 10

Thursday   11

Friday   12

Saturday   13

Sunday   14

APRIL 2024
Week 16

Monday   15

Tuesday   16

Wednesday 17

Thursday   18

Friday   19

Saturday   20

Sunday   21

APRIL 2024

Week 17

Monday   22

Tuesday   23

Wednesday 24

Thursday   25

Friday   26

Saturday   27

Sunday   28

APRIL 2024

Week 18

Monday 29

Tuesday 30

MAY 2024

Wednesday 1

Thursday 2

Friday 3

Saturday 4

Sunday 5

MAY 2024

Week 19

Monday   6

Tuesday   7

Wednesday   8

Thursday   9

Friday 10

Saturday 11

Sunday 12

MAY 2024

Week 20

Monday   **20**

Tuesday   **21**

Wednesday   **22**

Thursday   **23**

Friday 24

Saturday 25

Sunday 26

MAY 2024

Week 21

Monday   27

Tuesday   28

Wednesday 29

Thursday   30

Friday   31

JUNE 2024

Saturday   1

Sunday   2

JUNE 2024

Week 22

Monday   3

Tuesday   4

Wednesday   5

Thursday 6

Friday 7

Saturday 8

Sunday 9

JUNE 2024
Week 23

Monday   10

Tuesday   11

Wednesday 12

Thursday   13

Friday   **14**

Saturday   **15**

Sunday   **16**

JUNE 2024

Week 24

Monday   17

Tuesday   18

Wednesday 19

Thursday   20

Friday 21

Saturday 22

Sunday 23

JUNE 2024

Week 25

Monday   24

Tuesday   25

Wednesday 26

Thursday   27

Friday   **28**

Saturday   **29**

Sunday   **30**

JULY 2024
Week 26

Monday　1

Tuesday　2

Wednesday　3

Thursday　4

Friday   5

Saturday   6

Sunday   7

JULY 2024

Week 27

Monday   8

Tuesday   9

Wednesday 10

Thursday   11

Friday 12

Saturday 13

Sunday 14

JULY 2024

Week 28

Monday 15

Tuesday 16

Wednesday 17

Thursday 18

Friday   19

Saturday   20

Sunday   21

JULY 2024
Week 29

Monday   22

Tuesday   23

Wednesday 24

Thursday   25

Friday   **26**

Saturday   **27**

Sunday   **28**

JULY 2024
Week 30

Monday   29

Tuesday   30

Wednesday 31

AUGUST 2024

Thursday   1

Friday 2

Saturday 3

Sunday 4

AUGUST 2024

Week 31

Monday   5

Tuesday   6

Wednesday   7

Thursday   8

Friday 9

Saturday 10

Sunday 11

AUGUST 2024

Week 32

Monday   12

Tuesday   13

Wednesday 14

Thursday   15

Friday   16

Saturday   17

Sunday   18

AUGUST 2024
Week 33

Monday 19

Tuesday 20

Wednesday 21

Thursday 22

Friday   23

Saturday   24

Sunday   25

AUGUST 2024

Week 34

Monday 26

Tuesday 27

Wednesday 28

Thursday 29

Friday   **30**

Saturday   **31**

SEPTEMBER 2024

Sunday   **1**

SEPTEMBER 2024

Week 35

Monday 2

Tuesday 3

Wednesday 4

Thursday 5

Friday 6

Saturday 7

Sunday 8

SEPTEMBER 2024

Week 36

Monday   9

Tuesday   10

Wednesday 11

Thursday   12

Friday   **13**

Saturday   **14**

Sunday   **15**

SEPTEMBER 2024

Week 37

Monday   16

Tuesday   17

Wednesday 18

Thursday   19

Friday 20

Saturday 21

Sunday 22

SEPTEMBER 2024

Week 38

Monday   23

Tuesday   24

Wednesday 25

Thursday   26

Friday   **27**

Saturday   **28**

Sunday   **29**

SEPTEMBER 2024

Week 39

Monday   30

OCTOBER 2024

Tuesday   1

Wednesday   2

Thursday   3

Friday 4

Saturday 5

Sunday 6

OCTOBER 2024

Week 40

Monday   7

Tuesday   8

Wednesday   9

Thursday   10

Friday   **11**

Saturday   **12**

Sunday   **13**

OCTOBER 2024

Week 41

Monday   14

Tuesday   15

Wednesday 16

Thursday   17

Friday 18

Saturday 19

Sunday 20

OCTOBER 2024

Week 42

Monday   21

Tuesday   22

Wednesday 23

Thursday   24

Friday   25

Saturday   26

Sunday   27

OCTOBER 2024

Week 43

Monday   28

Tuesday   29

Wednesday 30

Thursday   31

NOVEMBER 2024

Friday   **1**

Saturday   **2**

Sunday   **3**

NOVEMBER 2024

Week 44

Monday 4

Tuesday 5

Wednesday 6

Thursday 7

Friday 8

Saturday 9

Sunday 10

NOVEMBER 2024

Week 45

Monday 11

Tuesday 12

Wednesday 13

Thursday 14

Friday   15

Saturday   16

Sunday   17

NOVEMBER 2024

Week 46

Monday   18

Tuesday   19

Wednesday 20

Thursday   21

Friday 22

Saturday 23

Sunday 24

NOVEMBER 2024

Week 47

Monday   25

Tuesday   26

Wednesday 27

Thursday   28

Friday   **29**

Saturday   **30**

DECEMBER 2024

Sunday   **1**

DECEMBER 2024

Week 48

Monday   2

Tuesday   3

Wednesday   4

Thursday   5

Friday 6

Saturday 7

Sunday 8

DECEMBER 2024

Week 49

Monday   9

Tuesday   10

Wednesday 11

Thursday   12

Friday   **13**

Saturday   **14**

Sunday   **15**

DECEMBER 2024

Week 50

Monday   16

Tuesday   17

Wednesday 18

Thursday   19

Friday   **20**

Saturday   **21**

Sunday   **22**

DECEMBER 2024

Week 51

Monday 23

Tuesday 24

Wednesday 25

Thursday 26

Friday 27

Saturday 28

Sunday 29

DECEMBER 2024

Week 52

Monday   30

Tuesday   31

JANUARY 2025

Wednesday   1

Thursday   2

Friday 3

Saturday 4

Sunday 5

NOTES

NOTES